GREEN IS THE COLOUR OF MEMORY

GREEN IS THE COLOUR OF MEMORY

HUZAIFA PANDIT

Hawakal Publishers

Published by Hawakal Publishers, 185 Kali Temple Road,
Nimta, Kolkata 700049

Email: info@hawakal.com

Website: www.hawakal.com

First edition (India): May, 2018
Copyright © Huzaifa Pandit 2018

Cover art: Pradnya Kushal
Cover designed by Chitrangi
Author photograph: Akram Ahmed

ISBN: 978-93-87883-09-3

Price: INR 220.00
USD 9.00

Dedicated to Mom and Hirra—
the everlasting presences in my life

REFLECTIONS OF PERSONAL MEMORIES

In Huzaifa Pandit's poetry, Kashmir is an expression of love, of hurt and a dream one chases for a life without violence and trauma. This collection is fresh and angry, and it also reverberates with intriguing metaphors. The title, *Green is the Colour of Memory*, courts resurgence, resurrection, newness of life and everlasting hope.

One reads through the collection and notes that Huzaifa is anxious and keen. He's from a Kashmir that mainland India only exoticizes but doesn't try to understand from the core. This poet is from the mountains, valleys, springs and rivers that have seen prolonged dark nights and not the dazzle of Bollywood silver screen as one from outside Kashmir would be made to believe. In the vein of the Kenyan writer Ngũgĩ wa Thiong'o who says "language is a war zone," Huzaifa brings to his language a similar strident urgency. At times his expressions are heightened and the metaphors bristling. Never for a moment though has the diction relapsed into sloganeering or abjectness.

Also, because Huzaifa draws deeply from traditions of resistance, global political history, and Kashmir's beloved native bards, his language and angst are lodged somewhere between the lyrical lament of an Agha Shahid Ali and the philosophical quirkiness of a Jorge Luis Borges. As critic Bruce King noted about Shahid Ali, that the latter's poetry are written around insecurity and "obsessions [with]...memory, death, history, family ancestors, nostalgia," Huzaifa's poetry too charts a similar curve. Moreover, they ask questions—at times difficult and uncomfortable ones for the establishment to answer.

City of dead lights, I can't be consoled
What if the army of desire resigned to defeat
abstains from night's siege? ("Reading Faiz on Deewali")

Huzaifa is scathing, albeit elegantly so. This being his first collection, he reaches out to the reader with a caustic grace:

In simpler words I will seek truth like Buddha
in even simpler words, I will doze on expensive plastic chairs
be robbed of nightmares and thank
overcrowded university conference rooms ("At a Seminar on Agha Shahid Ali")

The language in this book is startling, and the emotions delicate. Like Shahid Ali, Huzaifa's central style is *ghazal*esque, although he writes free verse deftly. The *ghazal* tradition in his writing defines not the meter, rhythm and rhyme scheme, but the nuanced evocation of experiences of a beleaguered life in Kashmir:

Grief comes calling
In hired pain written in expired prescriptions ("Friends in Grief")

The current political climate of mainland India vis-à-vis Kashmir, and day-to-day happenings that keep people barely on the brink of sanity find tongue-in-cheek mentions:

monologues combed in cold gardens revised with chillai-kalaan *walked with colonized cabbages on iron wheels* ("Amjad Majid")

The poems in this collection are political as well as personal. Huzaifa's senses are trained for recording political mishaps that have kept the people of Kashmir imprisoned for decades. At the same time, he brings in a fable-like atmosphere to his own experiences:

I sit in the steaming kitchen
And listen to snippets of conversation
Between simmering oil
and the cold refrigerator ("Autobiography")

If one thinks Huzaifa's work is all anguish, grief and loud political bickering, one would be missing out on the humor in his commentary:

The fat cat barked: A spade, a spade sir!
People who use spades, Sir don't belong to high society. ("The Cat and Shakespeare")

Jorge Luis Borges had said that the task of art is to transform what is continuously happening to us, to transform all these things into symbols, into music, into something which can last in man's memory. Reading

Huzaifa Pandit brings us closer to understanding this even when he seems sunk to despair:

The night blares yellow from the one eyed car
and strikes my nervous eyes in the dark ("Sketches from Memory")

According to Borges, these symbols could be "colors, forms or sounds. For a poet, the symbols are sounds and also words, fables, stories, poetry." For Huzaifa, the symbols are stirred with the reflections of personal memories:

Yellow reminds me of the lilies
That once grew on my father's grave. ("Sketches from Memory")

For all the sources he draws from, Huzaifa has a distinct style. He rebels with grace. His expressions are often intriguing and he indulges in wide ranging formal exercises. If there was a modern Kashmir to know, away from simply the anger, hurt and betrayal, it would be in *Green is the Colour of Memory*. For this poet, the art of writing is to invite readers in a conversation that will spring hope eternal for the sake of Kashmir, peace and life; we would like to become a part of this exchange.

Nabina Das

March, 2018
Hyderabad

PREFACE

In the summer of 2017 *Rhythm Divine Poets* initiated perhaps India's first ever poetry chapbook contest. This ambitious project to recognize and publish new and upcoming poets saw participation by poets from all over the world. It was followed by the arduous task of judging the manuscripts by three noted poets, Prof. Sanjukta Dasgupta, Dr. Sharmila Ray and Mr. Kushal Poddar. After almost a year-long process of longlisting and shortlisting the final results were declared in January 2018 where Huzaifa Pandit and Kripi Malviya came out winners. A cover art contest too was conducted which was judged by eminent painters Mr. Partha Roy and Mr. Sudhangsu Bandyopadhyay where the art works of Srijoni Manna, Pradnya Kushal and Niloy Kanti Biswas were declared the winners. Two of those three artworks form the cover images of the two chapbooks. *Rhythm Divine Poets* are fortunate to have the services of *Hawakal Publishers* who agreed to publish the two winners of this contest.

According to Sanjukta Dasgupta discovering new poetic talent was a matter of great excitement and joy because the contest has amply proved that poetry in English in the 21st century is journeying into unprecedented terrains. Sharmila Ray acknowledges that poetry cannot be judged but she was again amazed at the transformative powers of words hence language. Reading the poems she was teased, troubled, enlightened and joyous. She believes that poetry is a metaphor not only to express the reality we are in but it also helps to build how we perceive reality and in these trying times we need it more than ever. Kushal Poddar realized that poetry contest results are the result of a momentary avowal or denial, a bend in the river. Judging the chapbook contest was an opportunity to step outside his comfort zone as a reader.

Rhythm Divine Poets, co-founded by three Kolkata-based poets, Dr. Amit Shankar Saha, Sufia Khatoon and Anindita Bose, has over the period of three years since its inception, worked for the promotion of poetry through various activities like events, workshops, publications, and giving platforms to young and aspiring poets. Currently the group has three youth coordinators, Nikita Parik, Ruth Pal Chaudhuri and Sanjukta Sarkar, who work tirelessly to bring the vision of the group into a reality. The group has utilized the advantages of social networks like WhatsApp, Facebook and Blogs (http://rhythmdivinepoets.blogspot.in) to create the so-called "poetry scene" and the success of this poetry chapbook contest is evidence of that effort. The group thanks the judges, *Hawakal Publishers*, and all those who came in support of the endeavour. *Rhythm Divine Poets* wishes the two winning poets the very best in their poetic journey in life.

Rhythm Divine Poets
Calcutta

CONTENTS

ACKNOWLEDGEMENTS

The poem "A Kashmiri Fairy Tale" was first published in *Calliope*, "Autobiography" was published as "Old Man and the Breeze" in *Kashmir Lit*, "Train to Bombay" was published in *Papercuts*, "At the Cafes of your Memory" in *The Bombay Literary Magazine*, "Curfewed Friday" appeared in *Jaggery Lit* and the poems "Buhu sings an Elegy for Kashmir" and "Reading Faiz on Deewali" appeared in *Noble/gas Qtrly*. The poem "Sketches from Memory" appeared in an unrevised version as "Colors of Memory" in *Miraas*, "Miscarried Poem" too appeared first in *Miraas*. The poem "By the Nighted Road" appeared in an anthology *Bridges of Fate*, "His Master's Voice" appeared in an anthology titled *Read By, Written By* to accompany Bonniers Konsthall's exhibition 'The Image of War,' "Letters to Azaadi" was previously published in the anthology *Map Called Home* [Kitaab, Singapore (2018)]. The line, Green is the Colour of Memory, is the title of a poem by the same name by Randhir Khare. It also appears as a line in the same sequence in his book, *River Day*, published by Grasswork Books. I owe a special debt of gratitude to Asmet Mir and Deeba Sarmad for their unflinching support over the years. I am grateful to Nabina Das for writing the foreword, Jhilmil, Saima and Linda for the blurbs. I am also thankful to Sunita Ticku, Neerja Matoo, Nighat Fatima, Hameeda Nayeem, Ather Zia, Sahana Mukherjee, Amjad Majid, Minakshi Watts and Bhawna Kak for their belief in me over the years. I am grateful to Richa Singh who has been an invaluable source of love and blessings. I am indebted to my two creative writing professors: R Raj Rao, and Randhir Khare at the University of Pune. Last but not the least, I am grateful to *Rhythm Divine Poets*, and *Hawakal Publishers* for publishing my first book.

A KASHMIRI FAIRY TALE

One day when there are no half-wet black clouds
in the warm blue sky
We will quarrel bitterly
and never agree with the other-
We will iron all our wrinkled adjectives
and dress to dine on fresh arguments.
We will put on redrawn maps
sewn from gaudy geography.

We will fold our positions carefully
and tuck them neatly in our checked pockets
near our broken rib-caged heart.
A dash of hesitant reflection
on the silly jokes to be made.
We will tune our voice chords
to just the right frequency for broadcasting
our politically incorrect verbs written in correct tenses.
We will wear chic shoes
fashioned from the leather of lazy history.
We shall walk in directions decided in divine dreams:
Thus spoke God who knew no sutra:
The barbarians have finally come
to bury you in brick domes painted
In the golden shadows of deaf twilight
near wooden bridges to rotten history.

That day, we will bake our metaphors
in kilns of warm warm tempers.
Green green grass will dance in the drowsy sun
of warm warm May
we will quarrel and quibble night and day.

TRAIN TO BOMBAY

Puffing out the stench of tobacco,
maladies and middle class sweat oiling
grey working class hairs, the train
reluctantly shrugged off

tracks clothed in half grown grass
fed on human faeces,
shoving across slums
nailed to sprawling public lands
towards masses
stacked like humid logs
in decaying concrete jungles

Sun scorched skins of
scarred slums blurred past
while my dreams stuttered
into hazy nightmare ports
echoing shrill whistles and mock laments
of young men bred upon
regular exhibitions of pauper misery.

The *khakeed* snack vendors drilled my ribs
With their shrill cries
And hammered me into
the cramped corners
Like *wada* sandwiched
into a *pav*
to thread their way
past me in the crammed car.
I bargained peace with

ragged blind peddlers
selling balls flashing bright
lights of varied colours.

My imported accent
smelt of foreign currency,
yet I offered only a few stale
words of polite pity
I forgot all the memories
of high school geography
so forfeited my right
to feign nationality.
Would they slap betrayal if I confessed
my fair skin and brown hair were
painted by the icicles of Kashmir
rather than the European sun?
Alighting at the city, I stumbled against
paralyzed dreams crawling with timeless urgency.
Culture, the old beggar said, is ordinary.

READING FAIZ ON DEEWALI

The dim afternoon dozes
skin a hazy tint of mudded turmeric

It wakes with a sudden jerk
at the bored call of a black crow.

and runs in a drunk staggering gait,
trampling grass charred by the winter sun
into a lazy silence dripping from the sky
like an intravenous solution from a poisoned bottle.

Up on the fog-stained sky loom half knit clouds
like an overheard babble
of heartbroken sighs, dry blood and destitute tears.
The policed world is a torn web of an ossified
huntsman spider.

Beneath this cloak of fog
lies hidden the lost city of dead lights.

City of dead lights, who will draw the map to the prison
of exiled lights?

Is the prison guarded not guarded by foul empty tracts
and the horned ghosts fed
on briars and brambles in our blasted houses.

The humiliated army of desire
snores in total resignation on imported beds of shame.

City of dead lights, I can't be consoled:
What if the army of desire resigned to defeat
abstains from night's siege?

Lord bless your dead sweet hearts. Call upon them to
convey:
When their lamps are lit tonight, let high wicks be on
display.

CURFEWED FRIDAY

Things were different once.
The cleft sky wouldn't burden
my leaking skull.
During the famine of addresses
I inhabited some square feet.

In this city of lights
who would've imagined
gassed darkness would reign?
This nightmare had never hit me.
Had the suspicion ever struck you?

Many rains rain.
One even flooded TRPs
and an ungrateful people.
But the scarred blood stains
aren't wiped from sutured Jhelum
or bruised blue apple shells.

Now, your beloved is barricaded
in meshed screens of silence
it has been a century.
Once, when the city spoke a language
He was the *muezzin*.

AT A SEMINAR ON AGHA SHAHID ALI

The sky is a cremated mirror
I wish for avant-garde metaphors stolen from surreal
world

I want just the right mix: three spoonful of false similes
sprinkled with an autistic metaphor
plagiarized from cosmopolitan internet

I will ask the snoring cobbler to stitch
 the skeleton of my poem with threads of my memory

A hysteric conversation on match making
for a long decomposed poet
reeks of nostalgia for half-digested cigarettes

The very old theatric microphone
bows to old departmental academic claps
the speaker stammers American-Cashmere
an idea strikes my mind, a feeling arises in my heart

In the near future I may explore the country
without computerized post offices
for undelivered orgasms of chaste epistemology

In simpler words I will seek truth like Buddha
in even simpler words, I will doze on expensive plastic
chairs
be robbed of nightmares and thank
overcrowded university conference rooms

I know I want to write a poem, but the futility of it
I can't read, you can't write

EVENINGS OF DESPAIR

What does one do when the howling sky
mocks the brackish evening?

What does one do when the roof of a stale hospital
stares from my immodest window?

What does one do when dead flowers sprinkle
expired adhesives over faded dreams?

What does one do when portraits of ancestors
spew expired invectives at you?

What does one do when plastic rainbows
pellet your lamenting lungs?

What does one do when amputated houses
grate against wilted coffins?

FRIENDS IN GRIEF

Grief comes calling
in virgin 'harissa' mornings clad in baked iron.

Grief comes calling
in recorded messages of nostalgia in curfewed city.

Grief comes calling
in delirious fights against dysfunctional continents.

Grief comes calling
in midnight confessions of abandoned shame.

Grief comes calling
in hybrid horrors of tragic conversation.

Grief comes calling
in imagined voices in the cannibalistic world.

Grief comes calling
in hired pain written in expired prescriptions.

Grief comes calling
in unstable ethics of genetic discursivity.

Grief comes calling
in blasphemed love for debated serenity.

Grief comes calling
in schizophrenia and painted tea.

BEADED DREAMS

In an old nightmare
bitter bile concocted from rotten dreams
is stamped on our parched teeth
and broken necks.

We hum melodies
from monochrome funerals
where pale-eyed henna almonds
grace the groom's sutured hands.

We drift off to sleep
over shards of a shattered elegy
revealed to the Prophet of Unicorns.

We wake to midnight news:
Every dreamer
shall forthwith be considered a state enemy.

IMAGINARY HOMELANDS

When I mourn the loss of our imaginary homeland
drawn in the puddles of grey rain
fleeing from a furious monsoon.

I pour my exiled grief pressed close to my damp heart
into a well-thumbed copy of *The Namesake*.

Many encounters ago it lost its virginity
to my curiosity aroused from hearsay
deaf to oriental grief in the printed breath of Ashima.

At the coarse touch of pirated paper
I relive an old memory:
sixteen crescents ago, I consoled her namesake
in a drowsy car warm with a Kashmiri afternoon sun.

I grieved over her exiled grief
sketched in sudden tears and sullen eyes.

I bookmark the page with a tired sigh and play
a *ghazal* by Zafar
Will someone light a candle in the sovereign's defeated
memory on a modest grave in a foreign-land?

The wanderer darns the frayed threads
of an imagined memory.

AMJAD MAJID

monologues skimmed from polluted Jhelum
murdered near *Tatoo ground*
gunned ghosts of braying donkeys
occupied by forged guns

monologues embroidered on skinned Jhelum
and unmusical guitar trees
recorded on puddles of cold tea
and puritan new year parties

monologues combed in cold gardens revised with
chillai-kalaan *
walked with colonized cabbages on iron wheels
cut from crossbred ink-art journals
gifted to confused Kashmiri mannequins

monologues drank on faux news
in empty avant-garde cafes competing with a suffering
prophet
nailed on contested heritage
darned from illiterate memory

monologues smoked on geometric sermons
hermeneutics of poetic blasphemy
invoked by wrinkled mania in soiled parking lots
by a peer reviewed Chinese impostor

Note: *Chillai-kalaan* is the harshest spell of winter in
Kashmir that lasts for forty days.

27

AUTOBIOGRAPHY

I could never taste
The purple fire that decayed
On the thorn less roses
That lay strangely inert to the loud sneeze
Of the *maghrib azaan*
Peeled off from the cold sun
Itching from the damp blanket
Of the pale clouds
Emptied of all steel colored rain.

I could never hear
Fully the lisping breeze
When it injects the garden weeds
With drowsy epilepsy
And they scream off the phantasmagoria
Bred in bedded drugged asylums
That dot the summer plagued city.

I have often tried to touch
The overgrown pine trees
And their bare brown bones
That protrude beneath bottle green flesh.
But I could never store
Their black silhouettes in my skin memory
All my poor sketches were burnt
And surreal photos confiscated
for authentic forgery.

I have rarely tried to examine
The minutiae of the navy blue sky.

When I tried yesterday evening
And the evening last cold September
And the blue snowing December
I found the sole pinkish magenta bird
Circling, wailing, hungry
Pecking at the barren ashen clouds
For that date buried by history
When the wise old crows
Cursed it a curse
The length of a crawling century.

I sit in the steaming kitchen
And listen to snippets of conversation
Between simmering oil
and the cold refrigerator.
They talk about the blue thin wires
that transmit misled emotions
to the circuit of cognitive penury.

Here I am an old man
Waiting for the warm day to sink
At the rusted gates of the old cemetery
crafted in my memory.

ALONG CAME THE SOFT RAIN

I lie with my hollow face perpendicular to
the warm night sky
all its stars locked in my rat infested cupboard.

I have lain on my back since many millennia
studying the broad faced evergreen leaves
stapled on the dead charcoal trees.
The prophecies written on these leaves
have been read to me
by high priests who knew the yellow god.

I commit the fading prophecies
to a leaking memory
before they are lost to the men
who sleep like piled tiles
torn down from an old monastery.

The breeze carries the scent of fresh wet logs
burnt by the electrocuted ghosts
that haunt the slithering cracks
of the padlocked brick house
that houses my nightmares.

Lying very night against the uprooted banyan tree
I taste my brackish dreams
and touch the puddles of soft rain
dreaming of a fulfilled prophecy.

DREAMS AT MIDNIGHT

Often, on cold grainy midnights I wake up
to plaster my termite infested eyes
with a few rags torn from the blind night.

Muttering a profane prayer
I amputate a vial of cacti blood preserved
on my striped neck and fling
it over the depraved moon
that it might contract black death.

The beige moon exposes the clandestine poems
scratched with blunt scalpels
on the maimed hill by fallen angels
dead from muffled laughter.

Often on cold grainy midnights
my delirious ghost is chased
across the barren land and sinks
in the cold, slimy mud
mouthing an old forgotten song:
You haven't yet grasped the art of secrecy
How will you hide from me?

Often, on cold grainy midnights
the flag of your memory unfurls
on the mast of tedious death.

The doctor says
hysterics suffer from reminiscences.

THE CAT AND SHAKESPEARE

The bored black cat cornered the bald
-ing Shakespeare. So Mister Pear, Where did
thou do thy PhD? Poor Shakespeare! Poor, Poor
Shakespeare!
Felt his head itch, And thought: The cat is a bit
-ch. A really really mean wit
-ch. He thought on his feet, Queen
 Elizabeth's academy. Long ago, your maj-
-esty! I forget:14th or 15th or 17th cent-
-ury. The cat groped and poked er poor sec
-retary: Miss Memory and finally resigned:
Which year was it recognized by UGC?
What NAAC grade did you say, please?
The bored black cat cornered a sad Shakespeare:
S0 Mister Some pair? What did you write your PhD on?
Poor Shakespeare! Poor, Poor Shakespeare
In the ahistorical silence, he heard the wall clock tick: tick,
tick, tick
but no idea would come, nothing that'd click:
Elizabethan Tragedy, your Majesty!
The cat picked her crooked nose: I like only absurd com-
-edy. Shakespeare felt his old mouth twitch.
What an old cranky bitch! You see, your Majesty
I too wrote comedy, Full of fools with irony-
They called a spade a spade....
The fat cat barked: A spade, a spade sir!
People who use spades, Sir don't belong to high society.
Mr Orange pear...Don't interrupt sir. I hardly care...
I'll report my recommendation to the selection
committee.

SKETCHES FROM MEMORY

Green is the colour of memory specked
with shades of yellow grey

that walks along the twisted road
leading to the weeded lake

Choked by shallow depth and silent land
murmuring in watery pain

A rotten leaf fallen from a parched tree
is carried to cold eternity

frog croaks its last rites on the winding road
littered with memory

chains my cold feet with tired resignation.

Red is the colour of memory
That is perched on that twig

Where the bats offer blood
to the dazed ripe fruits

that fall dazed to the ground
drunk on the blood-wine

tender complexion bruised with soft wounds.

Grey is the colour of memory
That lies below the grey clouds,

Reflected in the sombre concrete
Gravel skinned boiled in tar

Heat locked in its heart and the joints of my knees.

Yellow is the colour of memory
That springs from the stooped street light

Bitten by moths, stung by butterflies,
Waging a lonely battle against the dark night

The night blares yellow from the one eyed car
and strikes my nervous eyes in the dark

Yellow reminds me of the lilies
That once grew on my father's grave.

BY THE NIGHTED ROAD

I may sleep today in the ditch
    By
      the
        sloping road
              Lit by the pale crescent
        Wrap the dizzy shadows
Of the dozing trees
        And dream of the bronze moon
                    Waxing

and waning
besides me
    I may ask the aged banyan tree
        That stares intently
           Bosom
        heaving from the thrill
        Of the damp

breeze
Does it
understand the
gentle agony
that plagues
me
in silken
      webs
of despair?
I may ask
about my remedy
today
Or I might just fall asleep

AT THE MENTAL HOSPITAL, SRINAGAR

Stay puzzled awhile
won't you?
Sketch the colours of the nightmare
on black nights
Paint the faint
shadows of dull grey memories
that now broker wry smiles:
concrete convictions painted
griefs ago
in watery pale fantasies.

Stay puzzled awhile.
Let the hands of the clock
hold the degrees of mystery
in the geometrical angles
drawn on square clocks.
What could be the story besides this?

Just a passing thought
puzzles me.
Did I not sleep all those nights believing
that there was an account
of the moments I spent
to purchase the
days from nights?
Stay puzzled awhile:
when lights were snuffed out
could they be heard sighing?
Stay puzzled a while-
I will multiply

reality by fantasy
divide it in time and space.

Bear with me a while
I will soon vomit memory.

THE MAD BOOK THIEF

If I were a mad mad thief
what would I steal?
What would I plot wrapped in the silhouette
of the savage moon?

What would I scheme
when the fidgety ash of an ill spent decade
rebels against the yawning poet who writes
with wrenched twigs on baked clay?

I'll read for inspiration
the drowsy dance of faded worms
that wrinkle the torn pages
Of an out of print edition of Biography of Lunacy
bound in placid velvet.
I noticed the edition yesterday
on a stale shelf creaking with sewn death
while robbing a locked library.

I threatened the librarian's old ghost
To credit the book to my long closed account.
She refused flatly in a loud baritone voice
On grounds of ineligibility.

I pleaded I have acted out long monologues
in boorish classes of bored philosophy.
She would not be convinced, I surrendered
all pretence of feigned sanity.

AFTERNOONS AT GOLAY HALL

The glum afternoon glows in the sweat beads
of a pale tube light fitted into the cold brick walls
Of a hall baptised after a man long dead.

The light soon settles upon the portrait
of the man with spectacled eyes
musing in time-worn colours at the missing letters
on his golden brass nameplate.
Perhaps the missing memories of his history.

The large table fan steals
an occasional suspicious glance
denying every history.
It rotates its blade lips
in a torrent of expletives
at the circular wooden table
with a deep crack in its midst
that houses a substitute history.

I peer and pore with the voyeur's delight
at the bland gaze of the square wall clock
frozen at twenty past four
AM or PM – it hardly knows.

Time, it whispers, was crucified
when lips were sealed
in three colours
and the nation collided with its destiny.

CURFEWED THIRSTS

how shall i garland the massacres?
on sale, doled out
colour shirt
blood stains
scent memory
kiss of tastes
left on hungry lips
how shall these stains
compose melody
vomit
empty sighs and sour sweat
how should i kindle my blood
spat from ulcerated mouths
stuffed with tumours

slit veins lie against the flesh—
emptied of life
what shall i pour into pyre
that lights funereal city?
how shall i write the epitaph
on graves dug on walls?

what shall i pour into cup
slake the corpse's thirst
veins run dry—
filled with venom
of serpent dreams

forbear from my body
with cacti acacia poison buds in it

shit out on leper scabs
no one feels thirsty.

MISCARRIED POEM

After such knowledge, what forgiveness?

I wash my fasting sins
with blood drawn from our square mirror.

Its glass heart blurts an old Bollywood *geet*:
A pauper's version of an unwept eulogy:

Raju lived on one square dream a day -
Raju will be The Raj Saab, some distant day.

Raju - cine Malgudi guide,
Imaginary geography, musical forgery

Drought bitten death sprawled on the sandy shore,
Awaiting reincarnation.

When I was young, they claimed
reincarnation is a myth.

Else wouldn't poems sprout in my room?
Exhumed elegies of euthanized dreams
and buried ballads of barren love.

I, a miscarried poem, will my epitaph:
"As flies to wanton men, are we to th' poets.
They kill us for their fun."

LETTERS TO AZAADI

Yaa tera tazkira karay har shakhs
Ya hum say koi guftgaoo na karay—Anonymous

They barricade us, dear
in halls of censored silence.

A half dead rumour
whispers you will visit soon.

Black roses
shed mourning, buds
bulge in the blind garden
beside frantic beds in the fort-prison.

We
were directed to forget
the taste of tulips left on battered
tongues and further directed to report
the rumours of your exile to stinking Dal.

We
wrote back
An ember breeds in our ancestral mouths
when cold minutes prey on a mutilated memory.
We wrote that this fire also feeds on our caned bones.

We
Remain wedded to our delusion:
One day, the final destination of mirages
will testify in courts of reality. Their apprehensions

too will be dismissed, we too will wheel in the hollow
horse of victory.

We
are still prisoners of the sorcerers.
They lure us with outlawed remedies and handcuffed
potions. They gouge out our warm heartbeats and
auction them
at the loud borders over feasts of rented revelry. We
are yet foolish dear
to smuggle letters to you in our beats. Do they reach
you? Did you read them?

HIS MASTER'S VOICE

(For Major Avtar Singh—assassin of Kashmiri Human
Rights lawyer, Jaleel Andrabi)

Master,
they play your voice
at night on the broken
gramophone when the light worms
have slept, tired of the drenched morning
that never ends.

Master
Your notes shake hands
like the fleeting rain falling on
blown out lamps. The days are sad, Master
yet at night smoke of sadder death fills my wide
nostrils.
They burn all the idols
of gods anointed by
 you.

Master
I petition to dye
The soiled bowl of moon
with the warm tint of that fateful
spring.
Master, I petition
the shadows of banned stars
protest at night near my tongue tied window and break
open
my last

heart.
Master
I have forfeited my dogmas
surrendered every charade of a plan.
I have sworn via costly affidavits before
their Lordships: I won't atone my sins.
Yet, every night, Master, my throat refuses to howl.
I ache for
a sip of warm
blood.

Master
curse my sad eyes.
Your murderer left the house
weeping and wailing. I never consoled
him. He cupped your warm blood in his coarse hands
and deposited it softly in my
bowl. The taste lingers,
Master. How can I then
set you
free?

MINUTES OF A MEETING

Neither a ritual of friendship, nor any mark of enmity
Both adopt a similar colour in your city.— Khatir Gaznavi

Look, did nobody inform you?
The vultures meet tomorrow to discuss the magpie.
The feast is set and the guests are met, in Coleridge's
words.
Today, the radio news announced the magpie stands
accused
of slander, misinformation and rebellion against the
dead summer.
The summer was found dangling upside down from the
almond bough
in the masked gardens yesterday. The Magpie is the
prime suspect.
Yesterday, the radio declared it in four dead languages
every hour.
I heard them.

Indeed, did nobody inform you?
They have all the proofs. The magpie was found
hopping in blood coated feet between the words
of a poem by Shahid. You know Shahid? No, not the
boy shot dead
yesterday. No, not the one they picked up last year!
No, Shahid – our beloved witness and cashmere poet.
The magpie was caught near his villas of peace.
The spotlight caught him
eying the inscriptions on the graves
recently whitewashed. We need new symbols,

they announced on the radio. So, they have wiped
hurried blood
off the clichéd inscriptions. You know the elegy
about the swallow returning the garden back to the
gulcheen – the black rose thief.
The radio announced elegies are banned now.
I heard them.

Indeed, did nobody inform you?
That the trial is due soon. The magpie has spilled the
beans.
It is due to be grand conspiracy. The bats have shut
their bored eyes.
They have seen and heard enough. No prior sanction is
required to display
its gassed innards on the clock tower. The radio
threatened miscreants to not expect mercy.
I heard them.

Indeed, did nobody inform you?
Last winter, the magpies hung in the warm jails
were piled on the blasted road. They wrapped them in
smoked shrouds
after calculating the price of a censored massacre. Their
ghosts have promised
to immolate themselves at the feast in protest. The
wary vultures have announced
that nobody shall be permitted to take any liberty, so
they will step up security.
The radio speculated it remains to be seen who
emerges the victor.
I heard them.

THE MANUAL OF OCCUPATION

Woh kehtay hain ranjish ki baatain bhulade
mohabbat karay, khush rahay, muskurade —Akhter Sheerani

We are ordered to forget, forgive
love, smile and stay happy.

We are ordered to forget, forgive
bury dirges in naïve graves.

We are ordered to forget, forgive
scheme feverish curfew.

We are ordered to forget, forgive
console the polite brutes.

We are ordered to forget, forgive
wreck our stuttering memory.

We are ordered to forget, forgive
rob hours from cleft palms.

We are ordered to forget, forgive
wrap concertina wire around bored necks.

We are ordered to forget, forgive
bulldoze shrines of memory.

A GHAZAL FOR ZAHID

(Killed by Indian forces in Chadoora)

Thunder, sand, foam, froth
Run away from my garden alas!
Tears, laments, poems, blood

At work my colleague whispers our brother is dead
His last words were great is the sorrow of night

Harassed hearts char in black bullet smoke
In hollow graves great is the sorrow of night

In the desert shrine, pilgrims stone scheming Iblees
Lord we testify great is the sorrow of night

In the dreams of fading Ishmael
Abraham says son, great is the sorrow of night

When wrinkled nights kiss gassed coffins
Choked chinars yell great is the sorrow of night.

Exile us to hell stoked by national fantasy
In heaven great is the sorrow of night.

BUHU SINGS AN ELEGY FOR KASHMIR

Your forgotten sorrows
now trickle into the heart thus
Like idols who visit desecrated temples
After their slaughter.

Persuade the night of separation
not to tarry any longer
The heart already aches a little less,
Your memory too teases no longer.

We lack the intellect to reciprocate a favour
else she arrives, determined to do us a favour—Faiz

Buhu sings *sighra aaween sawal yaar*
Call out to your dead lovers a little longer.

The beloved weeps in a hollow tongue
Smear condolences with meaning a little longer.

We know the law, and all the statutes
Let the murderer deceive us a little longer.

Amulets hang from black coffins
Untie half-burnt promises a little longer.

We promise to bare heads in *mehshar*
Command the last sun to beat down a little longer

Spill scented ink, and bury brocade paper
Bear the drought of good poems a little longer.

Notes:

Sighra aaween sanwal yaar. Come quickly, dark handsome love

Mehshar. day of judgement.

Buhu is a Sufi poet who wrote in sairaki

TESTIMONY IN FEBRUARY

Murdering a lover was never far from any beloved's mind-
but before your regime, it wasn't the general practise—Dard

Faraz, what befell the garden's residents this time?
Why don't my friends of the cage answer me?—Ahmed Faraz

We will evacuate our grief
Won't you rent our empty hearts?

We will forsake our creed
Won't you be the Prophet of heresy?

We will prevail upon Death
Won't you outbid it at the auction?

We have disowned desire
Won't you accept our turn of phrase?

We forgot your name
Won't you silence our conversations?

We scheme we will be faithful
Won't you seduce us in sore custody?

We have abandoned our homes
Won't you house us in mirrors of history?

We gaze out from the prison window
Won't you blow out green stars and the moon?

We too call caged friends, Faraz
Won't they reply with tidings of a massacre?

ON VISITING MY OLD CLASSROOM

I grew up aimlessly
and too slow.

I might be aeging
for light fades quickly.

Yet I have harboured
a notion of an art.

As I grew up
I numbered my years.

I still keep those numbers
and stare at them.

They lie besides me
for old ghosts

do pay a visit, sometimes
to their graves.

AN OLD PHOTO ALBUM

I know the difference between rhyme and rhythm
so scavenge old photographs

Dozing in musty shelves
of creaking cupboards

With an old broken tape recorder
to record their autobiography.

After coughing up an hour or two
I find a whiskered brown mouse

Sewn in my new red handkerchief
and lick his stained blood.

yet, the photos never speak to me.

DEATH IN FEBRUARY

(For the Sopore Encounter that claimed five lives)

Once upon an everyday death,
February snow wears a cold night
in its blinded eyes, and sets out to meet
fellow occupants of fresh obituaries in stale
newspapers.

Obituaries
that seek asylum from winter drought
in lost *samovars* of salted tea served with warm butter
at funerals of young militants to thirsty mourners.

Thirsty mourners
sit across each other in opaque tents
and lay bets on average velocity of new guns
being tested in old defense factories sewn on frenetic
metropolis.

They dust off
a dead militant's arithmetic
books lying in sealed schoolbags
to find formulae for exact square area of elegies
cast by the hill-shrine on *malkhah* in which threads
tied on its latticed windows will be given a state burial.

Their elegiac areas never agree
So they bargain a lump-sum settlement
of dinners over smelly kerosene evenings

and grainy news on BBC Urdu Radio. They hasten to sign
affidavits that declare on phone-in programs that the sorrow
of love was only a ruse, we were fated to suffer, and
suffer our destiny.

Notes:
Malkhah: largest graveyard in Kashmir located at the foot of Hari-Parbat Hill.
Samovar: a Large copper kettle used in Kashmir to serve hot tea.

AT THE CAFES OF YOUR MEMORY

Faiz, what befell the fellow travelers of late last night?
Where did the morning breeze halt?
Where did morning alight?—Faiz Ahmed Faiz

At an avant-garde café in uptown Pune
the reserved tables celebrate
a teenager's birthday in cosmopolitan English.

My nearly dead phone flares up with a call from home:
My mother laments in frayed kashmiri:
I am happy you aren't home, two boys
were shot dead today.

The waiter sprinkles stale fury over my posh coffee
and computes the rushed sum of gunned death
on pale margins of an old novel
once read by my dead father:
Not a Penny Less, Not a Penny more.

The ghost of the balloon
that blew itself up like an old bomb blast
yesterday in the market
of my cowering poems incites me:
Stab the cricket babble,
set fire to the uncaring bids of cricketers,
bend the expensive cutlery of showy fashion
and split the pleased table of long-lived puberty.

My mother is so grateful I am safe and alive.
I am her world and her afterworld.

I must not argue about Kashmir; I must
keep safe. She suspects my poems are unsafe
and wants them shipped to her without delay.

The door of our house is blocked
by the tent set up by a timeworn *hartal* to celebrate
the death anniversary of Republic of Tricolored-Death.
The stiff tent will be led to the *mazaar* tomorrow—
Brown bamboo bones packed neatly in coffin-white
canvas.
The courier will then reach me.

She drops the dead phone. I rise and pay my overdue
bill,
shake the birthday boy's surprised hand,
smile politely, and wish him a long life ahead.

BEDSIDE TALES FROM KASHMIR

The Native American on the spotted brown horse
had never heard of Big Bad wolf and Red Riding hood.

The Native American on the spotted brown horse
stoked a dry fire and cursed his godfathers in heaven.

The Native American on the spotted brown horse
murmured Hiawatha slayed the big brown mountain bear.

The Native American on the spotted brown horse
set out to fight with blades of pointed yellow grass.

The Native American on the spotted brown horse
met the Big Bad wolf and his bag of empty tricks.

The Native American on the spotted brown horse
sought consolation from his horse's blistered hooves.

The Native American on the spotted brown horse
sculpted raw runes on the wolf's curved teeth.

The Native American on the spotted brown horse
heard the last red ghost croon in his mangled chest.

The Native American on the spotted brown horse
shuddered at the ghost's bleak elegy.

The Native American on the spotted brown horse
never knew of Big Bad Wolf and Little Red Riding Hood.

GETTING LOST IN PUNE

roads in translation conspire in sly tongues against me
                monsoons of plastic mannequins on
sale dupe me

i walked up to the hitchhiking highway
                driven by humid hoardings that
advertise cosy homes

and asked for the mud-red state bus
                that outraces the graveled trees.

sheaves of blue acid rain wriggle
                under my skin and drench my
perspiring voice

 the *brahmin peths* warn
                buses never arrive in the late rains

tea over the corner radio blares Mukesh:

                if only Time hadn't revoked
                our vows of infidelity

                You'd have possessed me.

                like others, i too would enjoy
                the favour of your company

PLASTIC SILENCES

In a plastic silence
we listen
to plagiarized dramatic monologues

watching, sneering
as the stage lights up
for another tragicomedy
suffering
from compulsive obsessive boredom.

We scribble invectives
on bits of paper
recovered from pedestrian cigarette stubs
fresh from foul mouths
spat on constipated toilet floors.

We dream of vomiting
our imagined grief
in dark perspiring class rooms
only for the tubes to shout bright light
denying us the pleasure
of one last absolute catharsis.

We listen
in plastic silence
to the confused monody of incoherent
snippets
of farcical conversations conducted
by square solitaire cards
installed on our forfeited cell phones

We listen
to coded transmissions
transmitted through molten plastic water bottles
held close to our cracked ribs.

HYSTERIA

I clench cold blue pebbles
in my swollen palms.

Mother sprinkles warm breath
gathered from drenched Quran and her prayer rug.

Uncle says four witnesses testified—
moon rose in Iqbal's medicated eyes on Eid.

He ploughed the soiled lane
with thirsty nails after the last bullet.

In the fresh *mazaar*, we bound his dead
feet with narcissus plucked from beside the grave.

The parchment of my heart
is empty, quite empty.

www.ingramcontent.com/pod-product-compliance
Lightning Source LLC
Chambersburg PA
CBHW020340130626
46549CB00003B/1230